THE TRUTH ABOUT EARLY AMERICAN HISTORY

THE TRUTH ABOUT THE FOUNDING FATHERS

CHARLOTTE TAYLOR

Please visit our website, www.enslow.com. For a free color catalog of all our high-quality books, call toll free 1-800-398-2504 or fax 1-877-980-4454.

Library of Congress Cataloging-in-Publication Data

Names: Taylor, Charlotte, 1978- author.
Title: The truth about the Founding Fathers / Charlotte Taylor.
Description: New York : Enslow Publishing, 2023. | Series: The truth about
  early American history | Includes bibliographical references and index.
Identifiers: LCCN 2022000271 (print) | LCCN 2022000272 (ebook) | ISBN
  9781978527966 (library binding) | ISBN 9781978527942 (paperback) | ISBN
  9781978527959 (set) | ISBN 9781978527973 (ebook)
Subjects: LCSH: Founding Fathers of the United States–Juvenile literature.
Classification: LCC E221 .T39 2023 (print) | LCC E221 (ebook) | DDC
  973.3092/2–dc23/eng/20220105
LC record available at https://lccn.loc.gov/2022000271
LC ebook record available at https://lccn.loc.gov/2022000272

Published in 2023 by
Enslow Publishing
29 E. 21st Street
New York, NY 10010

Portions of this work were originally authored by Ryan Nagelhout and published as *George Washington Didn't Have Wooden Teeth: Exposing Myths About the Founding Fathers*. All new material in this edition was authored by Charlotte Taylor.

Designer: Rachel Rising
Editor: Megan Quick

Photo credits: Cover, p. 4 North Wind Picture Archives / Alamy Stock Photo; Cover, pp. 1-6, 8, 10, 12, 14, 16-20, 21 22-24, 26, 28, 30-32 pashabo/ Shutterstock.com; Cover, pp. 1-6, 8, 10, 12, 14, 16-20, 21 22-24, 26, 28, 30-32 orangeberry/Shutterstock.com; Cover, pp. 1-6, 8, 10, 12, 14, 16-20, 21 22-24, 26, 28, 30-32 iulias/Shutterstock.com; Cover Brian A Jackson/Shutterstock.com; Cover, 1, 3, 5, 6, 8, 10, 12, 14, 17, 19, 20, 23, 24, 26, 28, 30-32 Epifantsev/Shutterstock. com; pp. 5, 9 Everett Collection/Shutterstock.com; p. 7 https://commons.wikimedia.org/wiki/File:Stuart-george-washington-constable-1797.jpg; p. 11 https://commons. wikimedia.org/wiki/File:Life_of_George_Washington,_Deathbed.jpg; p. 13 Science History Images / Alamy Stock Photo; pp. 15, 27 s_oleg/Shutterstock.com; p. 15 https:// commons.wikimedia.org/wiki/File:Poor_Richard_Almanack_1739.jpg; p. 17 https://commons.wikimedia.org/wiki/File:Patrick_henry.JPG; p. 18 https://en.wikipedia. org/wiki/File:L%27Enfant_plan.svg; p. 19 Miljan Mladenovic/Shutterstock.com; p. 20 ClassicStock / Alamy Stock Photo; p. 21 https://commons.wikimedia.org/wiki/ File:Thomas_Paine_by_Laurent_Dabos.jpg; p. 23 https://commons.wikimedia.org/wiki/File:John_Trumbull_-_The_Declaration_of_Independence,_July_4,_1776_-_1832.3_-_ Yale_University_Art_Gallery.jpg; p. 24 https://commons.wikimedia.org/wiki/File:Gilbert_Stuart,_Thomas_Jefferson,_c._1821,_NGA_69391.jpg; p. 25 N8Allen/Shutterstock. com; p. 26 https://commons.wikimedia.org/wiki/File:Jefferson_slaves.jpg; ; p. 29 https://commons.wikimedia.org/wiki/File:Scene_at_the_Signing_of_the_Constitution_of_ the_United_States.jpg.

CPSIA compliance information: Batch #CSENS23: For further information contact Enslow Publishing, New York, New York, at 1-800-398-2504.

Find us on

CONTENTS

WORDS IN THE GLOSSARY APPEAR IN **BOLD** TYPE
THE FIRST TIME THEY ARE USED IN THE TEXT.

THE MEN BEHIND THE MYTHS

In the late 1700s, America needed strong leaders. The men known as the Founding Fathers helped the original 13 colonies declare independence from England, fight a war, and build a new nation. You may have heard stories about people such as George Washington, Thomas Jefferson, and Ben Franklin. But are they all true?

The Founding Fathers helped the 13 North American British colonies become the United States of America.

Everyone enjoys interesting stories about important people. But sometimes facts get twisted around or forgotten over time. So, did George Washington really have wooden teeth or chop down a cherry tree? Let's take a look at the truth behind some familiar tales of America's Founding Fathers.

EXPLORE MORE!

THERE IS NO EXACT LIST OF FOUNDING FATHERS. A FEW WERE PRESIDENTS, BUT MOST WERE NOT. THEY WERE THE MEN WHO LED THE **AMERICAN REVOLUTION**. THEY CAME UP WITH THE IDEAS IN THE DECLARATION OF INDEPENDENCE. THEY CREATED THE GOVERNMENT THAT IS LAID OUT IN THE U.S. **CONSTITUTION**.

WASHINGTON'S TOOTH TROUBLE

Dental, or tooth, care in the 1700s was not like it is today. George Washington had many problems with his teeth. He said that they often hurt. They would fall out or had to be pulled out. He also had false teeth called dentures that were sometimes too big. But the popular story that they were wooden is untrue.

In Washington's day, dentists made dentures out of animal and human teeth, hippopotamus ivory, brass screws, lead, and gold wire. No one knows how the wooden teeth **myth** began, but it was even taught in schools for many years.

EXPLORE MORE!

BY THE TIME HE BECAME THE FIRST PRESIDENT OF THE UNITED STATES, GEORGE WASHINGTON ONLY HAD ONE REAL TOOTH LEFT. HE WORE DENTURES FOR THE REST OF HIS LIFE. THEY WERE VERY UNCOMFORTABLE AND MADE IT HARD FOR HIM TO SMILE OR LAUGH.

George Washington was known as a serious man. His mouth pain was part of the reason he rarely smiled.

THE CHERRY TREE TALE

One of the most well-known tales in U.S. history is about George Washington and a cherry tree. The story says that Washington was six years old when he chopped the tree down. He then told his father what he had done, stating, "I cannot tell a lie." The story was meant to show how honest Washington was. But it probably never happened.

A writer named Mason Locke Weems added the cherry tree story to his 1806 **biography** of Washington. However, earlier printings of the book do not contain the account. **Historians** have found no proof that it is true.

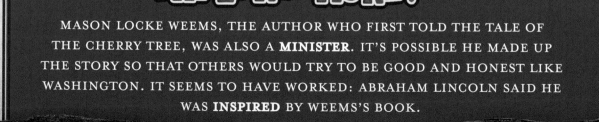

EXPLORE MORE!

MASON LOCKE WEEMS, THE AUTHOR WHO FIRST TOLD THE TALE OF THE CHERRY TREE, WAS ALSO A **MINISTER**. IT'S POSSIBLE HE MADE UP THE STORY SO THAT OTHERS WOULD TRY TO BE GOOD AND HONEST LIKE WASHINGTON. IT SEEMS TO HAVE WORKED: ABRAHAM LINCOLN SAID HE WAS **INSPIRED** BY WEEMS'S BOOK.

In the original story, Washington harmed the cherry tree, but he didn't chop it down.

DEAD OR ALIVE?

George Washington died on December 14, 1799. One story says that someone then tried to bring him back to life. This never happened, but someone did want to try! William Thornton, Washington's friend and doctor, was on his way to see Washington when he died. Thornton wanted to "attempt his **restoration**" with lamb's blood. He did not go through with his plan.

In Washington's time, some people worried about being buried before they were dead. Before he died, Washington asked his family and friends to wait three days before burying him, just in case he wasn't really dead.

EXPLORE MORE!

GEORGE WASHINGTON WENT HORSEBACK RIDING ON DECEMBER 12, 1799. IT WAS A COLD, WET DAY. WHEN HE GOT HOME, HE STAYED IN HIS WET CLOTHES SO HE WOULD NOT BE LATE FOR DINNER. HE SOON BEGAN TO FEEL ILL. TWO DAYS LATER HE WAS DEAD. WASHINGTON PROBABLY DIED OF A THROAT ILLNESS.

George Washington's final words were "'Tis well."

FRANKLIN FLIES A KITE

The most common answer to the question "Who discovered electricity?" is probably "Benjamin Franklin." Most people have heard the story of his "discovery" when his kite was hit by lightning during a storm. Actually, when this event happened, people already knew about electricity.

In June 1752, Franklin attached a key to a kite's string before flying it in a storm. He felt a charge on the key, proving that there was electricity in the air. Franklin's kite wasn't actually struck by lightning—he would have been killed! Electricity present in the air had traveled down the string to the key.

EXPLORE MORE!

BEN FRANKLIN WAS THE OLDEST PERSON TO SIGN THE U.S. CONSTITUTION. HE WAS ALSO THE ONLY FOUNDING FATHER TO SIGN THE DECLARATION OF INDEPENDENCE AND THE 1783 TREATY OF PARIS (ENDING THE REVOLUTION) AS WELL AS THE CONSTITUTION.

A painting shows Franklin with his kite and key. A scientist who tried to copy Franklin's **experiment** in 1753 was hit by lightning and died.

WORDS OF WISDOM

Ben Franklin had many interests and liked to share his ideas. He wrote a yearly guide known as an almanac under the name "Poor Richard." It was a book of advice and farming tips for the year. Many of the sayings from these books are still familiar today. But one of the most famous, "A penny saved is a penny earned," was not written by Franklin.

Franklin did write a piece of advice that is very similar to those well-known words: "A penny saved is two pence [pennies] clear." He meant that people who save money will have money to spend later.

EXPLORE MORE!

POOR RICHARD'S ALMANACK FIRST CAME OUT IN 1732. FRANKLIN WROTE ONE A YEAR FOR THE NEXT 25 YEARS. IN ADDITION TO ADVICE AND FARMING TIPS, THE GUIDES CONTAINED POEMS, RECIPES, AND WEATHER **FORECASTS**. AS MANY AS 10,000 COPIES WERE BOUGHT EACH YEAR.

Poor Richard, 1739.

AN

Almanack

For the Year of Christ

1739,

Being the Third after LEAP YEAR.

And makes since the Creation	Years
By the Account of the Eastern *Greeks*	7247
By the Latin Church, when ☉ ent. ♈	6938
By the Computation of *W. W.*	5748
By the *Roman* Chronology	5688
By the *Jewish* Rabbies	5500

Wherein is contained,

The Lunations, Eclipses, Judgment of the Weather, Spring Tides, Planets Motions & mutual Aspects, Sun and Moon's Rising and Setting, Length of Days, Time of High Water, Fairs, Courts, and observable Days.

Fitted to the Latitude of Forty Degrees, and a Meridian of Five Hours West from *London*, but may without sensible Error, serve all the adjacent Places, even from *Newfoundland* to *South-Carolina*.

By *RICHARD SAUNDERS*, Philom.

PHILADELPHIA:
Printed and sold by *B. FRANKLIN*, at the New Printing-Office near the Market.

A copy of *Poor Richard's Almanack* from 1739 shows the author as Richard Saunders, one of Franklin's many fake names.

HENRY'S FAMOUS WORDS

Patrick Henry helped inspire American colonists to fight for independence from England. It is widely thought that he cried, "Give me liberty or give me death!" in a speech at the Second Virginia Convention in Richmond, Virginia, on March 23, 1775. But this might not be true.

At the time, no one wrote down the speech Henry gave. Everyone agreed it was inspiring. But the famous words were not written down until William Wirt wrote Henry's biography 42 years later. Wirt asked others what they remembered, and he pieced the speech together. It's possible the words belong to Wirt, not Henry.

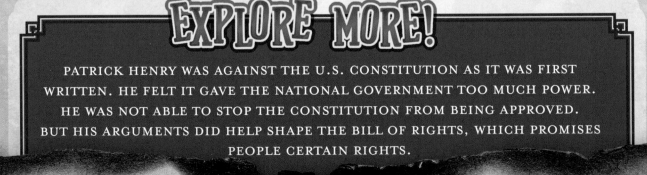

EXPLORE MORE!

PATRICK HENRY WAS AGAINST THE U.S. CONSTITUTION AS IT WAS FIRST WRITTEN. HE FELT IT GAVE THE NATIONAL GOVERNMENT TOO MUCH POWER. HE WAS NOT ABLE TO STOP THE CONSTITUTION FROM BEING APPROVED. BUT HIS ARGUMENTS DID HELP SHAPE THE BILL OF RIGHTS, WHICH PROMISES PEOPLE CERTAIN RIGHTS.

He may or may not have said "Give me liberty or give me death!" but Patrick Henry still fired up the colonists with his speeches.

WELCOME TO THE WHITE HOUSE

George Washington was the first president, so you might think he was also the first person to live in the White House. This was not the case. In fact, Washington was not alive when the White House was completed. It opened in 1800, about a year after he died.

This map shows the plan for Washington, DC, that was presented to George Washington in 1792. The city was named in his honor.

PLAN of the City of WASHINGTON.

George Town

POTOMAK RIVER

EASTERN BRANCH

Capitol 38: 53, N.

0: 0.

EARLY PLANS FOR WASHINGTON, DC

John Adams, the second president, was the first to live in the White House. He moved to Washington, DC, from Philadelphia, Pennsylvania, on June 3, 1800. The building wasn't finished yet, so he had to stay somewhere else for months. When Adams finally moved in, the White House still smelled like wet paint!

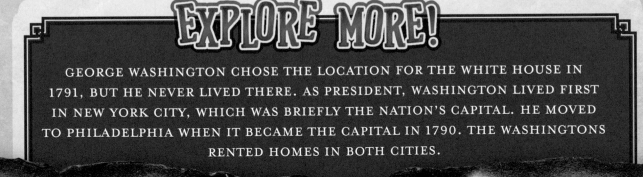

EXPLORE MORE!

GEORGE WASHINGTON CHOSE THE LOCATION FOR THE WHITE HOUSE IN 1791, BUT HE NEVER LIVED THERE. AS PRESIDENT, WASHINGTON LIVED FIRST IN NEW YORK CITY, WHICH WAS BRIEFLY THE NATION'S CAPITAL. HE MOVED TO PHILADELPHIA WHEN IT BECAME THE CAPITAL IN 1790. THE WASHINGTONS RENTED HOMES IN BOTH CITIES.

FRIENDS AND ENEMIES

The Founding Fathers were all important men who helped create the United States. You might suppose that they were friends who always agreed on how to run the country. However, many of the Founding Fathers didn't like each other. Alexander Hamilton, for example, was a **rival** to Thomas Jefferson, James Madison, and Aaron Burr. Hamilton died after a **duel** with Burr on July 11, 1804.

Aaron Burr (right) was the U.S. vice president when he killed Alexander Hamilton.

Thomas Paine wrote *Common Sense*, which argued for American freedom from England. He was once great friends with George Washington. But Paine later turned against Washington because he disagreed with Washington's actions as president.

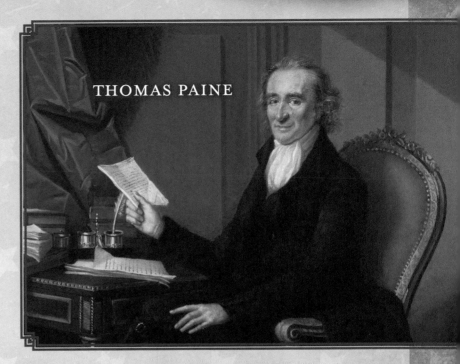

THOMAS PAINE

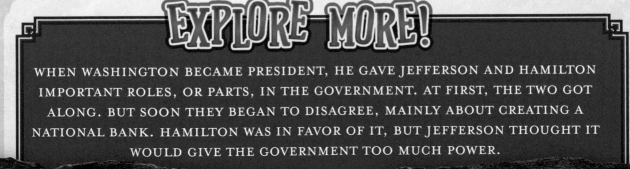

EXPLORE MORE!

WHEN WASHINGTON BECAME PRESIDENT, HE GAVE JEFFERSON AND HAMILTON IMPORTANT ROLES, OR PARTS, IN THE GOVERNMENT. AT FIRST, THE TWO GOT ALONG. BUT SOON THEY BEGAN TO DISAGREE, MAINLY ABOUT CREATING A NATIONAL BANK. HAMILTON WAS IN FAVOR OF IT, BUT JEFFERSON THOUGHT IT WOULD GIVE THE GOVERNMENT TOO MUCH POWER.

Thomas Jefferson and John Adams were another pair of Founding Fathers who had a rocky friendship. Many people believe that they were enemies their whole lives, but that is not true. In fact, they were good friends during the United States's early days.

Jefferson and Adams had different views on government. As president, Adams gave Jefferson's enemies positions in the government. Jefferson beat Adams in the presidential election of 1800. They stopped writing to each other. But after Jefferson's presidency, a friend pushed the two men to mend their friendship. They became close again, trading letters until they died.

EXPLORE MORE!

JEFFERSON AND ADAMS DIED ON THE SAME DAY: JULY 4, 1826. A COMMON MYTH SAYS THAT ADAMS WHISPERED, "JEFFERSON SURVIVES," IN THE MOMENTS BEFORE HE DIED. BUT THERE'S NO PROOF THIS HAPPENED. JEFFERSON ACTUALLY DIED A FEW HOURS BEFORE ADAMS.

Thomas Jefferson presents the Declaration of Independence in 1776. John Adams stands near Jefferson, hand on hip.

JEFFERSON'S MONEY MESS

Founding Fathers and former presidents were not always rich. Many people know that Thomas Jefferson had money problems at the end of his life. However, the story that he died penniless is untrue. Jefferson wasn't poor—he owned plenty of land. He did, however, owe a lot of money.

Thomas Jefferson owed about $107,000 when he died. That amount would be more than $2 million today.

Jefferson didn't make much money farming, and many people owed him money too. When those people died, he didn't get his money back. He also took on **debt** when his wife's father died. After Jefferson's death, his family had to sell much of his land, including his home, Monticello.

MONTICELLO

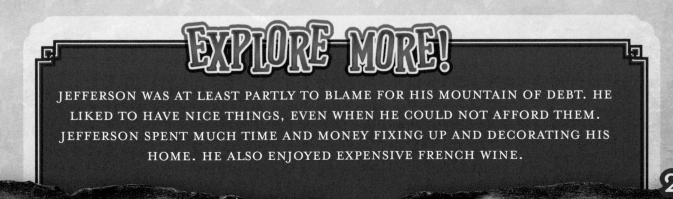

EXPLORE MORE!

JEFFERSON WAS AT LEAST PARTLY TO BLAME FOR HIS MOUNTAIN OF DEBT. HE LIKED TO HAVE NICE THINGS, EVEN WHEN HE COULD NOT AFFORD THEM. JEFFERSON SPENT MUCH TIME AND MONEY FIXING UP AND DECORATING HIS HOME. HE ALSO ENJOYED EXPENSIVE FRENCH WINE.

NOT ALL EQUAL

The Founding Fathers include the authors of the Declaration of Independence as well as the U.S. Constitution. The former stated that "all men are created equal." The goal of the latter was to give all Americans a voice in government. You might think, therefore, that the Founding Fathers were against slavery. This was not the case.

George Washington, Thomas Jefferson, James Madison, and Benjamin Franklin (to name a few) were all enslavers. They spoke and wrote about the evils of slavery. But this did not stop them from owning enslaved people themselves.

EXPLORE MORE!

GEORGE WASHINGTON HELD 123 ENSLAVED PEOPLE ON HIS FARMS WHEN HE DIED. IN HIS WILL, HE WROTE THAT HE WANTED THEM TO BE FREED AFTER HIS DEATH. BUT HE DID NOT WANT THEM FREED UNTIL AFTER HIS WIFE, MARTHA, ALSO DIED.

A page from a 1795 farm book lists 163 enslaved people at Monticello, Thomas Jefferson's home.

UNCOVERING THE TRUTH

The Founding Fathers were important men who played key roles in building the United States that we know today. They were also human: they had flaws, they got angry, and they made mistakes. It's important to understand both sides to get a full picture of who these men were.

There are many untrue stories about American history. When we hear a story many times, we often believe it. It's important to read and ask lots of questions to find out the truth about how the United States was formed. You might be surprised by what you learn.

EXPLORE MORE!

PAUL REVERE'S MIDNIGHT RIDE IS ONE OF THE MOST POPULAR MYTHS IN AMERICAN HISTORY. IN TRUTH, HE DIDN'T RIDE ALONE THROUGH LEXINGTON, MASSACHUSETTS, YELLING, "THE BRITISH ARE COMING!" THERE WERE OTHER RIDERS AS WELL. HE PROBABLY DIDN'T YELL, AND HE WOULD HAVE CALLED BRITISH SOLDIERS "REGULARS."

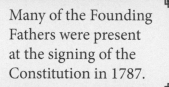

Many of the Founding Fathers were present at the signing of the Constitution in 1787.

George Washington

James Madison

Ben Franklin

Alexander Hamilton

GLOSSARY

American Revolution: The war in which the colonies won their freedom from England.

biography: The story of a person's life written by someone other than that person.

constitution: The basic laws by which a country or state is governed.

debt: The state of owing money.

duel: A fight between two people that includes weapons.

experiment: A scientific test in which you carry out a series of actions and watch what happens in order to learn about something.

forecast: An informed guess about future weather.

historian: Someone who studies history.

inspire: To cause someone to want to do something.

minister: A person who leads a church service.

myth: An idea or story that is believed by many people but that is not true.

restoration: The act of bringing something back.

rival: A person who tries to be more successful than another.

FOR MORE INFORMATION

BOOKS

Meltzer, Brad. *I Am Benjamin Franklin.* New York, NY: Dial Books, 2020.

Tarshis, Lauren. *I Survived the American Revolution, 1776.* New York, NY: Scholastic, 2017.

Trusiani, Lisa. *The Story of George Washington.* Emeryville, CA: Rockridge Press, 2020.

WEBSITES

Ducksters: American Revolution

www.ducksters.com/history/american_revolution.php

Check out fascinating facts about the American Revolution.

National Geographic Kids: Alexander Hamilton

kids.nationalgeographic.com/history/article/alexander-hamilton

Learn about Hamilton's accomplishments and tragic death.

Thomas Jefferson: The Declaration of Independence

www.americaslibrary.gov/aa/jefferson/aa_jefferson_declar_3.html

Find out more about the document that marked a new start for America.

INDEX